ENGLISH STYLE

SUZANNE SLESIN
AND STAFFORD CLIFF

PHOTOGRAPHS BY
KEN KIRKWOOD

CLARKSON POTTER/PUBLISHERS NEW YORK

Thank you again to all the people who allowed us to photograph their homes for English Style; *to our agent, Barbara Hogenson of the Lucy Kroll agency; Beth Gardiner, our editorial assistant; Ian Hammond, our art associate; Howard Klein, art director of Clarkson Potter, and Renato Stanisic; and our editor, Roy Finamore, who made sure that this new* English Style, *although smaller in size, was just as consistently strong as the original.*

Copyright © 1984, 1994 by Suzanne Slesin and Stafford Cliff.

Published by Clarkson N. Potter, Inc., 201 East 50th Street, New York, New York 10022.
Member of the Crown Publishing Group.
Random House, Inc. New York, Toronto, London, Sydney, Auckland.
CLARKSON N. POTTER, POTTER, and colophon are trademarks of Clarkson N. Potter, Inc.
Originally published by Clarkson N. Potter, Inc. in 1984.

Manufactured in China

Design by Renato Stanisic

Library of Congress Catalog Card Number 94-8648

ISBN 0-517-88215-9

10 9 8 7 6 5 4 3 2 1

Revised Edition

CONTENTS

INTRODUCTION

Classic English surroundings seem to embody almost everyone's idea of home. Hunting parties on country estates, teas in wood-paneled libraries, cozy weekends in bucolic picture-postcard thatch cottages set among colorful perennial flower gardens—all these idyllic and typically British scenes exist in both fiction and reality and all convey a sense of comfort, intimacy, and continuity.

The English country-house style owes its success both to its lack of artifice and to what the legendary 20th-century English decorator John Fowler termed "pleasing decay." Indeed, Fowler's gift has been described as an ability to re-create romantic interiors that have an uncontrived lived-in look. That sense of feeling secure and comfortable with the way the passage of time affects the surfaces and furnishings of a room is a hallmark of English style.

Being part of history and embracing a certain continuity are very English traits. The English have confidence in their past and both know and accept where they came from. But even those who did not experience the romanticism of the past seem eager to re-create it. The aficionados of a reinterpreted Victoriana are harking back to a past and a place that may not have existed for them at all.

The calm and more romantic English country-house look in its various guises has been one of England's most exportable interior design commodities, especially in the United States.

Like English manners and English literature, English design style has always had a particular appeal for those living abroad. And especially in the last decade, many notable American interior decorators have made international reputations reinterpreting the English country-house style in sophisticated Manhattan apartments and breezy weekend houses at the shore.

The rose-covered cottages, the kitchen dressers filled with blue-and-white china, the comfortable sofas upholstered in blowsy faded chintz, the scrubbed pine tables— are all decorating elements that promise an instant pedigree and have been adapted in part because of this appeal. A simple thatch cottage, for example, is preserved and *modernized. The well-worn stone on many back-door steps, where generations of cooks and housekeepers sharpened the kitchen knives, and the functional wooden latches that adorn the doors of rustic cottages are time-honored elements that rather than being eliminated are steadfastly guarded as important punctuation marks.*

But somehow, the classically British has managed not to become dull and repetitious. Although many houses and interiors are pleasantly familiar, they retain an individuality that has remained a hallmark of their continued vitality. In a country where overcast skies are a cliché born of experience, white walls, with their ability to reflect light, have become an accepted part of the decorating vernacular— and have proven to be an inspiring blank canvas for the idiosyncratic layering that remains one of the most enduring qualities of English decorating.

PRECEDING PAGES: *The comfortably furnished sitting room in David Mlinaric's country house is where family and friends gather.*

LOOKING OUTSIDE

ENGLAND has always been a country of individual houses and well-tended gardens, where privacy and a sense of self-containment are important elements. The urban building booms of the early part of this century, which produced rows of Victorian terrace houses, furnished city dwellers with thousands of one-family residences.

Many visitors to English cities can't fail to notice the rows of identical houses that line residential streets. The rhythmic repetition of these small-scaled buildings presents a comforting and secure scene. Indeed, one of the principal features of the English lifestyle is its uniformity. The polished brass knocker on the front door, the cozy morning room, and the neat garden are all components of a style that has become synonymous with the urban middle class.

There were few high-rise buildings in England until after World War II. Large-scale apartment buildings, although less rare, are still far from commonplace. It is these solidly built structures that in recent years have been divided into smaller units, which provide many of the flats that are typical of the English urban scene. And new and smaller versions of the stone and brick Victorian house, complete with many idiosyncratic details, are still being constructed because of the English attachment to the friendliness of this type of house.

The conversion of factory and commercial loft buildings into residential units is a more recent development, adding a new profile to the look of the domestic English façade. Loft living has come rather late to Britain, in part because the lack of housing was not an impetus, but also because of the basic English affinity for conservatism. In London, lofts are located in areas that often do not have the small-town neighborhood facilities—especially the small well-tended gardens and luxuriant public parks—that are so intricately woven into and deemed so necessary to English city dwellers, who no matter where they end up living always seem to dream of life in the country.

PRECEDING PAGES: *The row of identical gabled stone houses is a typical Cotswolds village scene.*

EXTERIORS

ABOVE: *Teviotdale, a neo-Georgian house of stone rubble covered with stucco, was built in upstate New York by Walter Livingston in 1773.* **PRECEDING PAGES:** *This thatch-roof stone house is the oldest in the village on the edge of the Cotswolds.*

16

ABOVE: *A long avenue of trees is a graceful introduction to a stately country house.*

RIGHT: *The red brick house in London was designed in 1868 by Philip Webb.* **BELOW RIGHT:** *The 1702 red brick house in South London was once occupied by John Francis Bentley, architect of the cathedral in Westminster.* **BELOW:** *The small-scaled building on an estate in Essex was once an aviary.*

ABOVE: *The exterior of the Norfolk farmhouse is of painted brick.*

ABOVE: *The main wing of the Sitwell mansion in Northamptonshire was added in 1777.*
LEFT: *The Georgian wing of a 1780 manor house in Sheffield has been converted into designer David Mellor's cutlery workshop.*

21

ABOVE: *The 17th-century thatch-roof farmhouse is set on a hill amid farmlands near Cambridge.* **RIGHT:** *A 1776 house, modeled after a Robert Adam design, is nestled among trees in Essex.*

23

A mid-19th-century tannery in London was converted into residential lofts by Michael Baumgarten, an American architectural designer.

ABOVE: *The row of 1830s town houses is typical of residential neighborhoods in South London.* **LEFT:** *A colonnade creates a rhythmic façade on London's Eaton Square.*

CLOCKWISE FROM TOP FAR LEFT:
The entrance to a house in the Spitalfields area of London is at the end of a narrow lane. Traditional stone balconies grace the front of a South London terrace house. Pots are filled with plants and flowers near the long 1830 colonnade of a house in Gloucestershire. The Albany, a prestigious 18th-century mansion converted to flats in 1804, is nestled just off London's Piccadilly. London's Tower Bridge can be glimpsed from the arched windows of a renovated loft.

The articulated roofscape is part of Felbrigg Hall, an early-17th-century Jacobean mansion in Norfolk, now a property of the National Trust.

ABOVE: *The Victorian house in London's South Kensington area was once the home of Edward Linley Sambourne, a cartoonist for* Punch *magazine. A glass window box is cantilevered out of the bay window in the dining room.* **LEFT:** *A traditional Victorian tile walkway leads up to the front door of a terrace house near the River Thames.*

ABOVE: *The main part of the sprawling house in Buckinghamshire dates from the early 16th century.* **RIGHT:** *A Victorian building that overlooks London's River Thames has been converted into residential lofts.*

ABOVE: *The understated brick apartment building dates from 1932.* **RIGHT:** *Rows of identical terrace houses are a typical sight in many English cities.*

The red brick country house was built as a hunting lodge in the second half of the 16th century. A fish-filled moat surrounds the house on all sides.

*The romanticism of the country
cottage is enhanced by the
roses encircling its front door.*

The Georgian east wing of a manor house was connected to a 16th-century building.

42

ABOVE: *The gray stone house was built around 1780 in the Oxfordshire Cotswolds.* **LEFT:** *A wrought-iron gate is set into a 1770 wall.* **FAR LEFT:** *A country house retains its timber-frame construction.*

GARDENS

RIGHT: *A beechwood arch is prominent in the garden of an Elizabethan house.* **BELOW:** *A hollyhock grows through a seat in an English-style garden in New York.* **PRECEDING PAGES:** *A flower-filled border frames a Cotswolds lawn.*

ABOVE: *The white-painted front gate is a charming introduction to a Victorian farmhouse in upstate New York.* **LEFT:** *A walkway of stones delineates a path through a vegetable garden.*

47

The statue of a hunting lady by Simon Verity, a modern sculptor, is a focal point among the trees in Rosemary and David Verey's garden.

49

ABOVE LEFT: *Benches are placed along the alley of lime trees in a garden in Gloucestershire.* **ABOVE RIGHT:** *A stable door opens onto the lawn of an estate in Essex.*

ABOVE LEFT: *The laburnum walk is one of the more recent plantings in a well-planned garden.* **ABOVE RIGHT:** *The design of the* potager *and its walks was based on plans in 17th-century English gardening books.*

A 100-year-old evergreen oak grows near the Gothic summer-house in Rosemary and David Verey's garden.

The late-18th-century classical temple was moved to the garden from a nearby park.

LOOKING INSIDE

THERE are those for whom the quintessential English interior will always be the grand country house with its enticing clutter, its well-worn upholstery, and its enviable patina of time. These are the rooms that result from years, if not centuries, of accumulation; layer upon layer of heirlooms; and mementos collected from a family's myriad experiences and travels abroad. These interiors can be read as if perusing a novel, with the objects representing multifaceted characters whose different roles contribute to the history of a room, even though they may be of little current significance on their own.

"While American interiors are often designed to provide an idealized picture of their owner's circumstances," said John Richardson in an article entitled "The Englishness of the English Country Look," "English interiors tend to tell the truth about people who live in them." That truth encompasses an ideal goal in decorating—a search for a well-heeled anonymity, a sense of continuity, and a style that is traditional and as hard to define as it is eccentric.

In a phrase that may typically sacrifice truth for effect,

but that could describe the appealing eccentricity of many English homes, Oscar Wilde said: "Only the great masters of style even succeed in being obscure." The individuals who create these personal interiors are the freest of designers. They do not rebel against existing conventions because they are simply not tied to them. That may be one of the reasons why even established contemporary interior designers in England today manage to keep their interiors from looking as if they were all out of a single mold.

English style today is a synthesis of various tendencies that reach back into the country's history and culture. Its contemporary interpretation not only respects the past but also seems to be in the process of presenting a new kind of pared-down image that is more in keeping with the 1990s. It is, not surprisingly, a rather understated design message. For all of its diversity of expression, English style, in its many guises, is first and foremost a livable style.

PRECEDING PAGE: *The library at Clandon Park, a stately residence at West Clandon, Surrey, boasts an ornate mantelpiece.*

LIVING

ABOVE LEFT: *A flower-painted screen stands near a door in a country house.* **ABOVE RIGHT:** *The flowers in the vase on the trompe l'oeil marble mantelpiece counterpoint those in a painting by Bill Jacklin.* **PRECEDING PAGES:** *Geoffrey Bennison, the late interior designer, created a play of textures in the 60-foot-long main living*

space of the London studio that once belonged to Sir Alfred
Munnings, an early-20th-century painter. **ABOVE LEFT:** *The stained-
glass window in the morning room of a Victorian house in London
has insets in the shape of family crests.* **ABOVE RIGHT:** *A throw by
textile designer Kaffe Fassett is draped over an armchair.*

62

ABOVE: *A 1919 landscape by Tom Mostyn hangs over a mantelpiece in a Chelsea residence.* **LEFT:** *Architect Piers Gough used a hairdresser's chair as one of the furnishings in the living area of a former World War I toy factory.*

ABOVE: *The blue walls of the library at Teviotdale, an American Georgian house, were inspired by one of the house's early occupants, steamboat inventor Robert Fulton.* **RIGHT:** *In the entrance of David Mlinaric's country house, coats and summer hats are hung on stags' antlers that wind up the wall.*

The top-floor bedroom, with its peeling plaster walls, in Dennis Severs's house in Spitalfields, London, re-creates a Dickensian atmosphere. The cane and bottle on the table mirror the objects in the drawing above the fireplace.

68

Above: *Oval paintings are symmetrically hung on either side of the fireplace in the red-walled living room of interior decorator David Hicks's London house.* **Left:** *A lavish draped bed sits in the center of the bedroom. The canopy and curtains are of 18th-century silk damask rewoven for Hicks.*

The huge drawing room in the Chelsea residence designed by Philip Webb in 1868 for G. T. Boyce, the Victorian watercolorist, has woven wool tapestry curtains that came from Blair Drummond Castle in Scotland. Fringed lampshades, tapestry-covered pillows, fur throws, and antique rugs, as well as an oversize Victorian sofa, complete the decor.

ABOVE: *The embossed wallpaper, lamps, overstuffed furniture, and knickknacks are all original Victorian details.* **LEFT:** *The sitting room of Dennis Severs's London house (seen through a ground-floor window) has been decorated in a Victorian style. The pictures are hung at an angle to cut down reflections in the glass.*

74

ABOVE: *In interior designer Philip Hooper's London flat, the sofa's loose cushions are covered in bits of fabric that the designer found in antiques shops.* **LEFT:** *In the hallway of interior decorator Lesley Astaire's country cottage, a 19th-century French mirror has been hung over a 19th-century carved Japanese settee.*

FAR LEFT: *Garlands of nuts add to the late-18th-century decor of a London drawing room.* **LEFT:** *A small table stands on the stenciled first-floor landing of a London house.* **BELOW:** *In interior decorator Mario Buatta's New York living room, antique dog paintings have been hung on sashes against walnut paneling that has been glazed in three shades of pistachio green.*

A large 18th-century Irish secretary stands in the sitting room of London interior decorator John Stefanidis's 17th-century house. The walls have been stenciled to look like faded silk.

A large painting by Owen Jones, a small painting by Stephen Buckley, and a sofa designed by Eileen Gray are part of the classic modern look of a London house.

LEFT: *In American writer Tricia Foley's country-style living room, the English theme is carried through with rusticated furniture.*
BELOW: *New York interior designer Mark Hampton created an English Regency period room in a Long Island mansion. Leather armchairs flank the fireplace in the green-walled gentleman's dressing room.*

CLOCKWISE FROM TOP FAR LEFT: *Chinese export china is grouped on an antique carpet–draped table. The white marble hall is one of Clandon Park's dramatic features. In John Stefanidis's London drawing room, the oak paneling has been painted white. A round convex mirror is the focus of the Victorian dining room. Chippy and Keith Irvine's winter drawing room in upstate New York was put together from bits and pieces collected over the years.*

DINING

ABOVE: *The antique chair in the dining area of a London loft once belonged to the 18th-century artist William Hogarth.* **RIGHT:** *Wicker and chestnut chairs surround a table in the informal breakfast area of Lesley Astaire's country house.* **PRECEDING PAGES:** *Creamware fills a niche in Stephen Long's candlelit dining room.*

*In the basement kitchen of
fabric designer Tricia Guild's
London town house, rattan
armchairs and a wooden
bench provide seating around
a long pine table.*

Guild's flea market and antiques shop finds of flower-decorated china by Clarice Cliff and her contemporaries are displayed on open shelves and fill a pine sideboard.

89

The early 18th century is mirrored in Dennis Severs's atmospherically candlelit and paneled dining room, where a half-finished glass of wine is on the table and a peruke has been left on the back of a chair.

92

FAR LEFT: *The pitched roof in London architect Piers Gough's loft made the top floor the most suitable to be used as a combination dining and living room.* **LEFT AND BELOW:** *Thonet bentwood chairs and a small sideboard are part of the simple scheme in the dining area in a London house.*

*Bits of old everyday china found at flea markets fill an old dresser
in the basement kitchen of a London house.*

The large eat-in kitchen of David Mlinaric's country house has uneven brick floors, a pine dresser, and a pine table.

A window seat covered in striped chintz, 17th-century Italian chairs, and a Queen Anne table provide a gracious place to dine in John Stefanidis's London flat.

ABOVE: *Candles burning in an 18th-century porcelain chandelier are reflected in the set of drawings by Millington Drake, an English artist.*
RIGHT: *A pair of late-18th-century Gothic bookcases stands in the windows of a terrace house that was decorated to recall the 1830s.*

98

100

ABOVE: *A cloth-covered table stands in the center of the hall that now doubles as a dining room on an estate in Essex.* **LEFT:** *A Thonet chair is set off by a suite of 1920s drawings by Natalia Gontcharova, a Russian artist.*

102

ABOVE: *Nineteenth-century fringed billiard-table lights hang over the dining table in an 1868 London house. The 1894 painting on the wall is 16 feet long.* **LEFT:** *One of Susan Collier's fabric designs serves as a tablecloth in the kitchen of her house in South London.*

COOKING

PRECEDING PAGES: *In Tricia Guild's London kitchen, well-used stainless steel pots hang in front of a patchwork of Victorian tiles.* **RIGHT:** *Large stockpots and other kitchen equipment are conveniently hung from hooks in the ceiling of a London loft.* **BELOW:** *In a country kitchen, pots, pans, and cooking equipment are stored on a wire rack above a butcher-block worktable by the stove.*

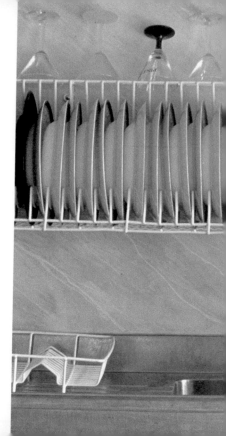

In the kitchen area of Piers Gough's loft, the wall and sink unit have been painted in marble trompe l'oeil by Paul and Janet Czainski. Dishes drip dry on a pair of racks.

ABOVE: *Herbs are hung to dry in a Victorian-era stone larder in a Queen Anne house in Wiltshire.* **LEFT:** *In the late 19th century, the fireplace in Dennis Severs's London house would have been used for both heating and cooking.*

The kitchen in a London house is as it would have looked about 1840. The open-hearth stove can still be used for cooking. The basement room is lit with candles.

RIGHT: *A coal stove with a small oven is used for warmth and some cooking in a restored 1915 caravan.* **FAR RIGHT:** *The open hearth is original to the kitchen at Clandon Park. On the door is a period rule book for the servants' hall that lists fines for transgressions and gives cleaning directions.*

Fiona MacCarthy and David Mellor's spacious kitchen takes up the center part of their Georgian house in Sheffield. A stainless steel sink is set into the natural English oak cabinets.

116

READING

ABOVE: *Books with decorative old bindings fill the low bookcases in the sitting room of a London house.* **PRECEDING PAGES:** *Thick pine shelves hold books of literature and history in art dealer John Kasmin's London house. An oak dining table doubles as a desk.*

BELOW: *A long curved wall filled with books provides an area for study in a London loft. The building was once a hat factory and warehouse.*

ABOVE LEFT: *Chicken wire painted in a crisscross design covers the fronts of the bookcases in a Norfolk farmhouse.* **ABOVE RIGHT:** *Books are crammed into two tall cases in a London bedroom.*

122

ABOVE LEFT: *A dresser on the half-stair of a London house has been arranged with old letters and books.* **ABOVE RIGHT:** *A wall of books rises behind the sofa in an artfully cluttered drawing room.*

ABOVE: *Leather-bound books form a backdrop to a Bokhara embroidery–covered table in John Stefanidis's sitting room. The drawing is by Matisse.*
RIGHT: *The walls of the Irvine library in upstate New York are papered in a tartan plaid. Pieces of antique china and figurines are interspersed with the books.*

124

ABOVE: *The attic ceiling in John Kasmin's London house was raised to allow the library to be installed under the roof. The walls are covered with photographs of writers by Man Ray.* **RIGHT:** *Books and boxes cover the desk in the small red-painted study of a farmhouse in Norfolk. Photographs of James Dean are stuck into the frame of an antique engraving.*

In the red sitting room—inspired by the famous red room in Sir John Soane's house—engravings that are not framed but glued to the wall are surrounded by printed borders, to give the effect of an 18th-century print room.

The mantelpiece, flanked by bookcases, has been painted in trompe l'oeil marble.

Two Indian Regency ebony chairs stand at either side of the faux-marbre fireplace. An antique French gilt clock is centered on the mantel. The floor-to-ceiling bookcases are filled with books on the decorative arts.

ABOVE: *A ladder stands near high bookshelves in the living room of a Norfolk farmhouse.*
LEFT: *In a London house, an 18th-century Gothic bookcase dominates a living room decorated to look as if it might have belonged to an early-19th-century antiquarian.*

134

LEFT AND ABOVE LEFT: *A portrait of Edith Sitwell by Pavel Tchelitchew hangs on the bookcases in the library at Weston Hall, an early-18th-century country mansion in Northamptonshire. The bookcase over the mantel holds antique leather-bound volumes.* **ABOVE RIGHT:** *Books are piled high both in front of and behind the comfy sofa in a country farmhouse.*

135

Vintage leather-bound books, piled on a small side table in the L-shaped drawing room of the house that once belonged to Punch cartoonist Edward Linley Sambourne and his wife, Mary Ann, add to the authentic decor.

Antiques dealer Stephen Long's London drawing room doubles as a library. Busts sit atop the bookcase that has been edged with faux tortoiseshell. The cluttered collections of books and ceramics give the room its rich textural look.

138

SLEEPING

PRECEDING PAGES: *A knubby bedspread and fabric-covered head-board define this 1930s-style bedroom in a London flat.* **RIGHT:** *A blue-and-white chintz called Tea Rose has been used for the walls as well as the canopy and curtains that surround Tricia Guild's lavishly dressed bed.* **BELOW:** *The bedroom is reflected in the mir-rored doors of a built-in storage closet. The Art Deco dressing table was made in the 1930s for an Indian maharani.*

ABOVE LEFT: *The elaborate canopy bed in the state bedroom is original to Clandon Park.* **ABOVE RIGHT:** *The brass headboard in a London gentleman's bedroom is typically Victorian.*

ABOVE LEFT: *The 100-year-old quilt was made by a group of women, members of a temperance league.* **ABOVE RIGHT:** *An American quilt covers a half-tester bed in a Norfolk farmhouse.*

An ornate Victorian sofa is displayed like a piece of sculpture
in this spacious bedroom in
Yorkshire.

A crewel-patterned fabric has been used to dress the bed in a former hunting lodge.

In a wood-beamed cottage bedroom, lace-trimmed pillows, a crocheted spread, and American quilts have been used on the bed.

The bedroom in a stone house has been furnished with a 1930s tubular steel bed and a table topped with a lace-trimmed cloth.

RIGHT AND BELOW: *In Susan Collier's London house, the paneling in the master bedroom has been painted blue. The quilt is sewn from pieces of Liberty fabric. The small chest of drawers is a turn-of-the-century English painted piece.* **FAR RIGHT:** *The bedcover in Philip Hooper's London flat was made from fabric silk-screened by Ann Collins in yellow, black, and ivory.*

152

LEFT: *The antique French box bed in a London loft has a headboard that looks like a huge picture frame.* **BELOW:** *The bed in John Stefanidis's London bedroom dates from the late 18th century, and the chaise longue is from the Regency period.*

ABOVE: *The boatman's cabin on Clive Evans's longboat has been decorated in the traditional way. Cooking, heating, and sleeping functions were imaginatively incorporated into the tiny area.*
RIGHT: *Doors below the box bed open to provide more sleeping accommodations.*

154

The pattern on the walls in Stephen Long's London bedroom was copied from an antique screen. Draped antique fabrics create a voluptuous headboard.

Diaphanous pale blue material that matches the walls encloses the bed in a London bedroom that was based on a Napoleonic theme. The columns and marble door frame are trompe l'oeil.

ABOVE: *An American wedding-ring quilt covers one of the Art Deco twin beds in a London loft.* **RIGHT:** *The heavily embroidered bedcover in a London bedroom dates from the 17th century.*

BATHING

ABOVE: *Although this bathroom in a Norfolk farmhouse was completely renovated, the original claw-footed bathtub was retained.*
RIGHT: *In a London loft, a freestanding bathtub has been installed near the bedroom area.* **PRECEDING PAGES:** *The mirrored wall behind the tub visually enlarges the bathroom in a London town house.*

166

LEFT: *In a country house, the sink has been set into a small wooden cabinet.* **BELOW LEFT:** *Tiles, painted in trompe l'oeil stencil by Mary McCarthy, are a feature of a country house bathroom.* **FAR LEFT:** *The walls in this spacious bathroom in a London house are painted an eau-de-nil color. The shelf, stool, and toilet seat are all mahogany. The photograph dates from the Victorian era.*

ABOVE: *A 1917 Gluck still life of lilies hangs in a London flat. The soft green marble used as the tub surround was part of a stock of old material.* **LEFT:** *The ground floor powder room in a historic Victorian house in London boasts the original marble-topped sink and fixtures.*

169

Original brass and porcelain
faucets adorn a vintage sink.

*The wash basin in a country
house was sculpted of wood.*

ABOVE LEFT: *In London, a French mirror hangs over an antique two-person bathtub in a guest room. The French porcelain taps have been set into the wall.* **ABOVE RIGHT:** *White marble is the material of choice for this bathroom in a renovated Queen Anne country house.* **LEFT:** *A collection of prints and photographs fills the corner above the bedroom washbasin in a Victorian powder room.*

COLLECTING

ABOVE: *A typical farmhouse dresser in a Wiltshire kitchen has been filled with blue-and-white china.* **LEFT:** *Antiques dealer Stephen Long has been collecting 19th-century white pottery boot warmers, here lined up on his faux-marbre mantelpiece, for years.* **PRECEDING PAGES:** *Susan Collier's collection of 1920s and 1930s ceramics was bought over the years with her housekeeping money.*

A well-choreographed lineup of Art Deco figurines and Wedgwood plates decorates the fireplace in a 200-year-old stone house.

William Gough Howell's collection of World War I memorabilia includes pins in the shape of airplane propellers, china, mock medals, political campaign buttons, and Flag Day flags. The model and toy airplanes are made of wood, brass, or tin. Housed in a

gallery at the architect's country house, the collection includes a vitrine filled with white china tanks, guns, and busts and a display case featuring model boats, miniature tanks, and Toby jugs that portray some of the important personalities of the period.

Household packaging and memorabilia, as well as old shop signs, fill a bookcase in a London apartment kitchen.

A wax model of Queen Victoria in her coronation robes and some Egyptian antiquities are displayed under glass domes on a table in the living room of a London museum curator.

The small fan-shaped guide board, leaning on a mid-17th-century black cabinet filled with curiosities, was copied from those used in stately homes to provide a key to the prints in the drawing room.

185

Some of textile designer Susan Collier's favorite creatures, such as crocodiles and bugs, are displayed on a Malaysian lacquer table. A frog-shaped jug by the potter Alice Britton, surrounded by seed-pods from all over the world, is the center of a still life of natural objects. Two ikats from Afghanistan act as a backdrop.

187

ABOVE: *Old glass containers, both plain and etched, are grouped on a shelf.* **RIGHT:** *Clear glasses, a coffeepot, and wine goblets—all both functional and decorative—are aligned on a shelf in a country kitchen.*

*In a London loft, two lamps
frame a colorful collection
of china, mostly from Portugal,
that is set out on a cake stand
that came from London's
Biba department store.*

190

Jugs and bottles are crowded above a small wall-hung cabinet that contains food in an old-fashioned London kitchen.

A theatrically assembled candlelit still life in a London house includes a quill, dried fruit, a cinnamon stick, and an old letter written on parchment.

John and Janie Newstead built a reproduction of a 1920s chemist's shop in the backyard of their house near Norwich and stocked it with authentic fixtures and bottles.

SPIR. AMPHOR. | SPIR. ETHER. NITR. | SPIR. VINI RECT. | TINCT. AURANTII | TINCT. GENT | TINCT. RH. CO. | TINCT. GENT. CO. | TINCT. QUINIÆ AMB | TINCT. RHEI

ACID. BORIC. | GUM. ACACIÆ | PULV. SAPONIS | PULV. GLYCYRRH. CO. | PULV. AMYLI | PULV. JALAPÆ | CARBO LIGNI | ROSE DENTIFRICE | CARBOLIC DENTIFRICE | PULV. ARECA

*Glass jars with Latin labels
are filled with such pharma-
ceutical necessities as boric
acid and powdered toothpaste.
Pills, including some marked
"poison," are also stored in
vintage jars.*

Large blue glass containers are lined up on the top shelf behind the counter and are offset by the vintage etched-glass panel. The meticulously displayed pharmaceuticals add to the authenticity of the collection.

Pill machines, suppository molds, as well as original light fixtures and display cases, advertising signs, prescription books in Latin, and certificates, have been assembled for the Newsteads' pharmacy, which is to be permanently installed in the Bridewell Museum in Norwich, England.

ABOVE: *Creamware is displayed and used in a London dining room.* **RIGHT:** *Cabbage-shaped porcelain and pottery and tulip-shaped Spode and Staffordshire chocolate cups are some of the pieces arrayed on the red lacquer Queen Anne secretary in Mario Buatta's New York living room.*

ABOVE: *A collection of shiny antique brass jelly molds is lined up on the dresser in the kitchen of a grand country house.* **RIGHT:** *A group of green glass bottles forms a striking composition against the speckle-finished wall in Tricia Guild's London house.*

The front hall at Weston Hall, an early-18th-century country mansion in Northamptonshire, is lined with bells that summoned servants to the different rooms. Part of a collection of swords hangs beneath.

ABOVE: *Pastel-colored vases by Keith Murray are grouped on open shelves in a London flat.*
RIGHT: *Hand-painted English Poole pottery, dating from 1925, is displayed in a painted bookcase.*

A LITTLE
STYLE
BOOK

JAPANESE
STYLE

SUZANNE SLESIN
STAFFORD CLIFF
DANIEL ROZENSZTROCH
PHOTOGRAPHED BY
GILLES DE CHABANEIX

A LITTLE
STYLE
BOOK

CARIBBEAN
STYLE

SUZANNE SLESIN
STAFFORD CLIFF
JACK BERTHELOT
MARTINE GAUMÉ
DANIEL ROZENSZTROCH
PHOTOGRAPHED BY
GILLES DE CHABANEIX

A LITTLE
STYLE
BOOK

FRENCH
STYLE

SUZANNE SLESIN
STAFFORD CLIFF
PHOTOGRAPHED BY
JACQUES DIRAND

Other titles in the series